STORY OF SELF

"What If I Miss?"

Eye Fixation Stops You Missing A Sitter

Richard Chapman

Business Email Address: alcoholismprevention@gmail.com

Book design by Ayokunle Samson

Table Of Contents

Preface

You are reading this self-help novel as a sportsman, perhaps unaware of the octopus's connection to sports such as football, golf, darts, snooker—and possibly others.

The theme is to highlight, for all psychologically unaware sportsmen, the magical importance of **fixated eyes** in their sport.

To uncover this braincell magic, you follow John's story... He visits the World Snooker Championship in North England, where he is dumbstruck by a world champion missing a sitter! This moment causes John a fanatical but rubbish snooker player—to become inattentive while driving south. He causes a fatal accident, is sent to prison, and attempts suicide twice. Then, a shift in his fortunes leads him to discover the power of fixated eyes in playing snooker.

Together with John, you will uncover the importance of **fixated eyes in snooker**, explained in plain English not the gobbledygook often associated with the word 'psychology'.

At the end of the story, you'll find examples of how 'fixated eyes' can be applied to football, golf, and darts. Oh, and if you want to improve your snooker but wear glasses—buy yourself a pair of *snooker glasses* (yes, they exist), and you'll find out why!

Chapter 1
He's Dead For Sure

He's dead for sure! Those eyes will live with me forever.

When I came round, there were ambulances and police cars galore. I was put in an ambulance and driven off… to hospital, I assumed.

The police visited me in hospital the next day. They asked me what had happened, so I just told them the truth:

"I was driving south on the motorway when I decided to overtake a larger, slower lorry into the second lane. Suddenly, I lost control of my lorry and cannoned into the central crash barrier, with my cabin facing north and my load facing south. Then I saw terrified eyes disappearing under my front wheels. I don't remember anything more than that."

"Your driving licence, please, sir."

"Confirm your name, please, sir."

"John Smith." He'd obviously done some work on my account. "You've been driving this lorry for ten years without causing an accident or ever being in one. Correct?"

"Correct."

"Same company?"

"Yes."

"Are you familiar with this motorway?"

"Very… I know it like the back of my hand."

"You are a very experienced and very good driver, so what distracted you? Don't tell me about any animals running into your path, etcetera, because there weren't any."

"No. It had to be the snow."

"Are you going to plead guilty or not guilty to dangerous driving that caused the death of someone?"

"Guilty. But it was the snow that made me lose control… except I hadn't noticed it settling so fast."

"But why didn't you notice the snow? There weren't any other similar accidents on that day."

"I was distracted. I was thinking of something else, which I shouldn't have been. I normally only let my mind wander when the road is empty. I know that 10 to 30% of accidents on motorways are caused by driver inattention. I've now become one of them, and I deserve whatever punishment comes with this horrific crime. It'll never leave my mind—the last look he had before his death. No one can forgive me for it, especially his family and friends. How am I going to apologise to them?"

"What were you thinking of, then, that was so important you forgot ten years of trouble-free driving?"

"I'm sorry, but it's very, very personal. I don't want to tell anyone about that."

Chapter 2

A World Champion Thinking "What If I Miss?"

My boss, knowing how keen I am on playing snooker, had given me a ticket someone else couldn't use—for the final of the World Snooker Championships, held every year in North England. He knew I was delivering goods to the area at that time.

It was a great match, but with an extraordinary ending. One of the players—who had been close to winning the championship in previous years—had an easy chance to win it there and then! On that shot! And yet, he missed *the sitter* and lost the world championship! The hall crumbled. No one could believe it. And me? Probably the worst player in the hall, I thought, *even I would have potted that.*

The thing is, whilst I love the game, because of my job, it's not easy to find time to play club snooker… and even when I am around, I'm simply not good enough to get into the team anyway—due to lack of practice.

And now… how could anyone world-class, earning a fabulous amount of money doing what they love, and practising every day, miss that easy pot? You have to concentrate on every shot. He must have lost concentration. Did he say to himself, *"What if I miss?"*

What I can't get my head around is—yes, *I* would say *"What if I miss?"* Possibly on every shot I made, just to avoid leaving it as easy meat for my opponent… but the expected World Champion?

Nahhhhh… something wrong there. What can it be?

Chapter 3

From Prison, to Hospital, to Open Prison

I got four years in prison and a ten-year driving ban—yet I went contentedly. I had left my house keys with my brother, Frank, to look after my flat, and I felt I was being punished fairly.

All prisons, I'd learnt, have libraries, and I had worked out that I could learn a lot through studying something—maybe become a lorry mechanic? After all, I wouldn't be able to drive again for some years, if not ever, as a lorry driver… who would employ me?

But I hadn't counted on not being accepted by the other prisoners. I won't go into sordid detail about the treatment I got—"because you are a murderer"—but after two years in prison, I'd tried to commit suicide twice.

On the second occasion, I was taken from the hospital, not back to my prison, but rather to an *Open Prison*. I'd never even heard of an Open Prison before.

β

I was taken to the Governor's Office and greeted by the Governor of the Open Prison with a smile and a handshake.

"Hello, Smith. Please, sit down."

"Thank you, sir."

"Welcome to our Open Prison, where you are to stay for the remainder of your sentence. All the other prisoners are here as part of their rehabilitation plan, in preparation for release. They're not staying very long… as you are. But all of you are considered low risk to the local community and extremely unlikely to simply disappear.

"You won't meet any of the other prisoners—they live in the large building on the other side of these grounds. This end is out of bounds for them, except when they come to see me.

"So, what's the difference for you, compared to where you've just come from? First, there is minimal security here, because none of you want to go back to normal prisons—should you try to run and get caught.

"Then, we allow you contact with the outside world, including your family. Prisoners spend most of their day away from prison, on licence, to carry out work, education or other resettlement purposes. Just remember to be back before ten at night.

"I see you have a brother, Frank—your sole relation—who happens, by chance, to live quite close to here. I hope you're on speaking terms with him?"

"Yes, sir. Thank you, sir."

"I'm looking forward to having you here, Smith, and I trust you'll enjoy it, too."

"Thank you, sir," I muttered, bewildered and dumbfounded, thinking I must be dreaming.

The Governor then stood up. I shot to attention like lightning, and he came round the end of his desk.

"John, I'm here to help you. When you've settled in, jot down any queries and just knock on the door. If I'm not available at that moment, we'll arrange another time."

I was simply *double* dumbfounded. I felt tears wanting to stream down my face. What a lovely man. Too good for prisons!

"You can go now—there's someone outside waiting to take you to your room and then show you around the premises."

I couldn't hold back my tears of joy any longer. They just poured out, and I was mopping them up as fast as I could. The Governor put his arm around me, ushering me to the door, saying gently: "Don't hold up your brother."

CHAPTER 4

Gay, as Well as a Raper?

Am I going mad? Why haven't I been sent back to that nightmare of a prison? Why would the Governor of any prison call me by my Christian name? Help! What did he say? *"I'm looking forward to having you here, Smith, and trust you will enjoy it, too."* Is he gay?

I'm not—but I also don't want to suffer prison rape ever again, whether the raper is gay or not. After my second attempt at suicide, they'd probably have taken my razor away and I'd have become known as *'the bearded murderer'*.

β

It was indeed Frank outside the door. We shared a bear hug, and he gave me a handkerchief to carry on the wipe-up.

"Don't say anything, John. Just let me take you to your room. Mine is next to yours."

As we got close to my room, I said, "Right at the end of a corridor! Must be to deaden the screams."

There was only one bed in my room—which was a blessing—and all my belongings from the hated prison were on the bed, too.

"I know, John. Let's go and get a drink and a sandwich and take them into the garden. There's a lovely table out there in this June sunshine…"

It wasn't until I'd downed a very welcome cup of tea and a sandwich that anything sensible came out of me:

"I can't tell you about what has happened to me, just yet. I can only think that if I could, I would gladly sit at this table in solitary confinement for the next two years, without talking to anyone… Silly, isn't it? Please tell me about you, Kitty and Alan. How are you doing since we last met?"

Nothing had changed. Frank—who was ten years older than me, at forty-five—now had a twenty-year-old son, Alan, working with him in his plumbing business. Kitty looked after the phone and the books. A successful little business with a good reputation.

"What about Susan, how's she doing?"

Susan was my only ever girlfriend, who'd preferred someone else a few years ago. She's the daughter of Kitty's best friend—old school pals.

"She's not married in between times. I can ask Kitty to find out for you."

"Yes, please. How much time have you got before you go home?"

"I'm not going home until tomorrow. The Governor gave me a ring the other day, asking if I could come here today and stay overnight to help you settle in."

"Amazing."

Chapter 5

The Snooker Table and a Dartboard

"I know what you'd like to see, John. Come this way."

Frank and I entered a large room with a full-sized snooker table and plenty of space around it! The biggest man in the world could enjoy playing here. Wow—am I going to be allowed to play snooker here? In a prison?

Memories of going to the World Championships flooded in, including those eyes.

Frank knew all about my visit to the World Snooker Championships and the accident that put me in prison—but he didn't know what had distracted me.

"Can you tell me, John, what had distracted you? I won't tell anyone else. Everyone's mystified."

"Not yet... please don't ask that again... Isn't this room amazing?"

β

After breakfast and saying goodbye to my brother—who had about a twenty-minute drive home—I went to see the snooker room again. Had it all been a dream?

There was no one there. If I'd believed in God, I would have gone down on my knees and thanked Him for my entry into paradise!

There was a rack of cues and other snooker equipment against the wall, and a tray of snooker balls on a table in the corner... with a chair beside it for me to sit occasionally... what more could I want? There was also a dartboard—and darts available!

I selected a cue, close in length and weight to the one I used to play with, and set up the balls to play a game. Then I heard footsteps coming towards the room. Ah? Someone wanting to challenge me?

It was the Governor.

"Good morning, Smith. Did you sleep well?"

"Yes, sir. So did my brother, sir. He's just left to drive home. It was extremely thoughtful of you, sir, to help me in that way. Thank you, sir."

"I've come to tell you I've found you a job! You've been accepted to work at the local library. We have a close link with the council, and they have certain jobs they reserve for our prisoners—ideal for those wanting a bit of extra money and experience of civvy street. If you don't like it—five mornings a week—come and see me, and I'll see if I can find you something else."

"Wow!"

"What are you doing here?"

"Oh, sorry, sir. Am I supposed to book the table? Or... or... am I out of bounds?"

"No, no, no, no. It's just that it hasn't been made use of before—and neither has the dartboard... well, to the extent I thought it would be. I was thinking of sending it to another Open Prison. But if you want to make use of it—or them—please do. Just shut that door over there, so as not to allow some locals to invite themselves in and cause us a problem. We're very careful not to upset the locals, but they are not allowed onto our grounds.

Any questions you've woken up with?"

"Yes, sir... but I'm frightened to ask you."

"Go on—you can ask me anything, and I won't count it against you."

"Phew! Thank you. I obviously expected to go back to my other prison, yet you said yesterday that I am to be here for the rest of my service. Are you sure... please... sir?"

"Absolutely sure. I have no knowledge of the reason for your coming, and it is the first time for me to be able to place someone here with your record. But I've taken an instant liking to you, and I don't expect to regret my acceptance of you here. I ask you only to stick to the rules: that you get back before ten and that you don't allow locals to come onto our property."

"I understand that perfectly, sir, and will abide by your rules at all times."

Chapter 6

What a Kind Governor

I had a wonderful day playing snooker against myself, changing my cue a couple of times before finding the right one for me. I liked winning—even if only against myself!

Then my days became a matter of going to the library to work five mornings a week, helping in the café, and, with the rest of my time—being summer—exploring the area on foot and practising snooker on my own.

My brother, Frank, called in one Saturday while I was setting up my snooker table. I went to the Governor and asked if it was alright for my brother to play snooker with me.

He gave me a wink.

"Living twenty minutes away by car means he's not a local. He's welcome to come any time he likes — if it's just you and he that play."

Frank was about the same standard as me. That is, if what we played could be called any recognised standard. Rubbish? Well, not quite—we tried our best. What was often happening was that we missed sitters! Fancy not potting a ball that was screaming to be pocketed! We also tended to hit the white ball so hard it went several times round the table… often ending up in a pocket itself! Now *that* was absolute rubbish.

After a couple of hours, I found another chair so that both of us could have a sit down. Frank was the first to get his breath back:

"You asked about Susan. Kitty spoke to Susan's mum... for about three hours, actually. God knows what they were talking about! But you'll like the outcome. Susan has asked me to take you back to her today to have a chat — and she'll bring you back here later."

What did I have to lose?

Only my place in the Open Prison, as it turned out.

β

"You bloody fool, you. You're going to have to go back to your other prison. What on earth made you stay out all last night? I told you that you had to be back here before ten—and you swore you would be. That meant 10 o'clock at *night*, not this morning! And you know it.

I can't imagine anything you could tell me that would help. But try me! Whatever you do, don't tell me a lie—I've heard them all before. Did you hear the National Anthem passing a house whilst running to catch the last bus, so stood to attention and missed it? That's an old one... forget it!"

I felt dumbstruck. I hadn't paid enough attention again. I *deserved* to go back to hell.

"Come on, Smith, there must have been a reason for it. You aren't stupid—and you have so much to lose."

I managed: "But as you say, sir, I broke the only rule you asked me to keep to." And then I burst into tears. My new, wonderful world had just been wiped out.

The Governor waited patiently for me to recover... even handing me an extra handkerchief.

"Go on."

"I met my old girlfriend, sir, who lives close to my brother's house. As you know, Frank and I played snooker here in the morning. My girlfriend promised to take me home for my brother..."

I choked and then recovered. "Sir, I suffered rape many times before I came to you—and I have always loved Susan..."

I began to cry again...

But managed to end with: "We... we... we fell asleep together."

There was a very, *very* long pause... and the Governor turned away from me. I heard a couple of sniffs and the blowing of a nose.

"Please don't send me back to hell, sir..."

Another pause.

"I promise it will never happen again, sir..."

The Governor then turned round, still wiping his tears away.

"Go to visit your Susan as often as you want to, Smith—but pay attention to the time... or you *will* go back to hell."

Chapter 7
Useless Library Books

In the town library, I was a helper to the person running the library's café. I didn't earn very much, but it was very quiet and peaceful. So different from my prison experiences! I had plenty of time to read a book I'd chosen from the library shelf—and pour myself a cup of free tea!

I'd taken a book called *Basic Snooker* to read, to see if it could give me any clues about the calamity at the World Championships. But no... absolutely not. I'd gone through that 'basics' level of play years ago. There was a statement that professionals go through their practice routines on their own, as if playing an actual match. Why? To concentrate solely, without distractions. *Hmm*, I thought... I can use this book to learn a few tricks I've never come across before, but otherwise, there was only one other thing that caught my eye: a professional player stepping back from taking his shot when someone coughed in the audience.

Hmmmm... So, if playing in a very intense moment, as the champion was, he should have stepped back because of the tension? Maybe. But I'd like to know more. Surely a champion should be able to cope with tension?

Could thinking *'What if I miss?'* cause him to miss that sitter?

β

I put the book back on the shelf and checked if there were any other books on snooker, but couldn't find any. So I went to the librarian for advice.

I explained the link between my accident and snooker, and said I wanted to find out what the psychology of snooker was—for example, how a professional player could miss a 'sitter'.

"You need to read *An Introduction to Psychology*. I'll bring it to you."

"Here you are. Can you bring me a cup of tea, please?"

Half an hour later, he returned with his empty cup to find me sitting on my stool, arms crossed, forehead furrowed like a field just ploughed by a tractor.

He leaned over the counter and saw my feet plonked on the book.

"Sorry, my shoes are clean. I was just about to bring it back to you."

"I was right then! I knew you'd need help with it, but I wanted you to recognise that for yourself. Your reaction is exactly the same as mine when I bought it for my subsidiary subject to English at university. I'd thought, *'Now's my chance to find out about the workings of my brain.'* But a quick glance nearly made me throw up! I very nearly dropped the subject right there and then. But I soldiered on. I gave it to you because I want you to understand just half of the chapter on *Attention*."

"I'm sorry, but it's all gobbledygook to me. I know a lot about *inattention*, because that's why I'm here. I'm sorry, but I know when I'm defeated."

"OK, forget the book for now. I'll explain the most important things to you—in English."

Chapter 8

Stick to Your Brain's Rules

"John, please call me Brian. Think of me as your best friend. Ask whatever you like, if you like. I did pass my degree in Psychology, but I've never practised it before—and I've never heard of its relationship to snooker. So, if I ask you about snooker, can you help me too, please?"

"Thank you, Brian, for that. It's lovely to feel like I'm talking to a friend... years ago... well, never mind. Yes, of course I'll help you as far as I'm able. I'm very keen on snooker, but I haven't exactly been successful in the past."

"Well, John, it's going to be my pleasure to try and explain where your brain helps you—without you needing to know *how it does it*! All you have to do is stick to your brain's rules… otherwise, you'll be forever missing a sitter!"

"Wow... really? Go on then, I can't wait to hear what you've got to say!"

"The potting of a ball in snooker would be classed as a *task* by your brain. And when you complete a task successfully—within its rules—it helps your future play because your brain, with the help of its army of 'messengers,' stores that memory within 2–3 seconds for later use."

"How does it do that?"

"I'm not going to tell you that because you'd just call it gobbledygook! But I'll tell you this: your brain has hundreds of billions of helpers, called messengers—or *neurons*, in psychology language—and they carry the information into your memory. And your memory, by the way, has the capacity to store hundreds of years' worth of 24-hour television programmes."

Brian smiled at me.

"Put your jaw back, John. Just don't worry about *how* your brain helps you—just obey the rules and enjoy the results."

"Ah, so, Brian… if anyone, even a snooker world champion, disobeyed the brain's rules, he could miss a sitter?"

"Exactly."

"Now I'm with you. What are the rules, then, Brian?"

"The rules depend on what kind of help you need with your snooker *task*. Luckily, in snooker, there's really only one task—which makes this much easier to explain. In snooker, your task is to hit the white ball with your cue, aiming it at the spot on the coloured ball to knock it into a pocket. Am I right?"

"I can help now! You're right. That white ball is called the *cue ball*, and the coloured ball is the *object ball*."

"Thank you, John. That makes it easier for me to picture what's happening. So, moving on—your brain controls the senses you need to use in potting a shot. Only those senses must be involved. Anything else becomes *noise*—which I'll explain in a moment. But first—of the five senses, which do you think are needed to complete the task?"

"Forgive me—but remind me what those five senses are?"

"Eyesight, hearing, touch, smell, and taste—usually listed in that order. So, which ones do you need to pot a ball? Do you need *all* of them?"

"Well, I can definitely do without smell, taste, and hearing. Eyesight is essential."

"What about touch?"

“Yes, of course—my hand has to operate the cue.”

“Great, John! So now we know: as long as your potting shot only uses your eyes and your touch on the cue, and it successfully moves the white cue ball to hit the coloured object ball—the very least you’ll have as a result is the saved shot in your memory for future use... as long as there’s no *noise* to stop it.”

“What noise, Brian?”

“Anything else. *Noise* can cause your brain to abandon its help. You glancing away… blinking, probably… the smell of a much-wanted cup of coffee… or a thought like *‘What if I miss?’* Or being flooded by tension and not paying attention. Even someone talking nearby or coughing in the audience at the wrong moment.

If any of the other senses—hearing, smell, or taste—interfere with the task, that becomes *noise*, and it can stop you from completing the task successfully.

What you’d call gobbledygook—and what I, as a psychologist, would call ‘neurological process’—is that the messenger, if your task is successfully completed, runs along your line of sight, through your eyes, and into your memory.”

“And that’s for use later!”

“You’ve got it!”

“Ah, Brian! So once again, you’re showing me how anyone—professional or amateur—could miss a shot. Whether easy or difficult.”

Chapter 9

Persistent Eye Fixation is the Winner!

"You, John, in snooker, need to use *Persistent Eye Fixation* every time you settle down to pot a ball—whether practising or playing. That means concentrating on the exact spot—the *target*—on the object ball you want to hit, and holding your gaze on it *throughout* the shot. From start to finish, your eyes must stay fixed. That way, no 'noise' will be powerful enough to distract you from your task. This greatly reduces the chances of missing a sitter."

"I understand, Brian. Well—I'm trying to! It's a lot to take in."

"Don't panic! Nobody absorbs all this in one go. But I hope you've grasped that this is *the most important* element in potting a ball—the one thing that can help prevent you from missing a sitter."

"I think so."

"Good. I've got two examples that'll help you really understand what *Persistent Eye Fixation* means. Ready, John?"

"Ready, Brian."

"Okay—imagine you're driving along a heavily congested motorway, and then traffic slows right down for about a mile. You're crawling along—but not at a complete stop. What do you think might be the cause?"

"There's probably a nasty accident on the other side of the barrier."

"Exactly. And how would you know if it's a *nasty* one?"

“Well, just guessing, but usually in really bad accidents, I don’t see any vehicles coming from the opposite direction.”

“Right. So, when you finally drive past the scene—slowly, like all the other cars—do you ignore it and focus solely on your own driving?”

“No, of course not. At that slow speed, I’d glance over at it—just like everyone else. That’s why traffic moves so slowly—everyone’s looking.”

“And when you glance… would you *prefer* to look longer, if you could?”

“Definitely. I might even want to stop and help.”

“Fair enough. What you’ve just described is *Persistent Eye Fixation*—when your eyes fixate on something, not necessarily knowing for how long. It becomes difficult to look away. Your attention is locked.”

“True.”

“Well, in snooker, *that* is what you must do every time you play a shot. From the moment you get down to play, your eyes must stay fixed on the exact point of the object ball you’re aiming for—right through to the end of the shot. That entire time span, from setup to contact, is variable—but your focus must remain constant. That’s Persistent Eye Fixation. And if you maintain it, no normal ‘noise’ will be able to interrupt your brain’s support for your shot.”

“Okay… I’m getting it.”

“My second example involves an eight-armed octopus! Stay with me—it’ll make sense in a second.

Imagine you’re walking beside a field filled with sheep and cattle… and suddenly, you see an *octopus* in the field.”

“What?!”

"Exactly! Your eyes would immediately become fixated on the octopus—because it's *so* unusual. And if you didn't have a time limit, you'd probably stare at it for ages, right? Wondering what the hell it was doing there… maybe thinking, *That dog won't help… Where's it from?* and so on."

"True. That would definitely get my attention."

"Right. The main feature of Persistent Eye Fixation is that your eyes can *stay locked on* something for as long as necessary. In snooker, this is powerful. When you're ready to shoot—and you've lined up your aim—you *must* lock your gaze on the exact spot of the object ball and keep it there from the beginning to the end of the task. Doing so cancels out external distractions, helps your brain complete the task, and guarantees that the shot—successful or not—is stored in your memory for future improvement.

In the octopus example, only something even more extraordinary could break that fixation. Like… another octopus joining it in the field!"

"So, you're saying the reason the champion missed that sitter could have been because he *didn't* use Persistent Eye Fixation?"

"Exactly. It's unlikely, but possible. Or maybe, for the first time in his life, the pressure overwhelmed him and he forgot to step back from the table and re-focus. It's also possible he just… didn't pay attention—like you did during your accident. And maybe, just like you, it was the first time he'd ever lost that focus in his professional life. Only he would truly know—and he'd probably prefer it *didn't* become public knowledge."

"So, what should I do?"

"This week, I want you to practise Persistent Eye Fixation—every time you line up a shot. From the moment you begin the task to the moment the cue ball strikes the object ball. Stay locked in."

"Thank you, Brian. I'm really looking forward to finally understanding what's happening 'behind the forehead scenes,' so to speak. And you've done a great job translating all that gobbledygook into plain English!"

"See you next week, John. And in the meantime, feel free to pop into my office to let me know how you're getting on."

"Thanks again, Brian. You've really got me thinking now—especially about those octopuses. Particularly if it was mating season!"

We both went on our way, laughing.

Chapter 10

Frank's Warm Seat!

When I got back, I immediately threw myself into practising *Persistent Eye Fixation*.

With unwavering concentration, I set to work—eager for Saturday morning when I could finally impress Frank with my improved play. No more missed sitters. No more misjudged angles. *Just clean, confident shots.*

Saturday morning was a disaster—for Frank.

I was far too good for him. For ninety percent of the morning, he sat on my chair, keeping it warm for the brief moments between my breaks. He hardly spoke a word, just sat there looking increasingly miserable as time passed. Each time he got up, it was only to miss a sitter or pot a red but fail to follow it up with another colour to start a break.

We finished early and sat together in silence, each of us quietly processing the situation.

"I'm sorry, John," Frank said at last. "I'm amazed at how good you've got in the three months we've been playing together. Good for you. It's clear you've had the time to practise, whereas I'm a working man—I come here to relax with you. Honestly, I've never practised snooker on my own… and I can't imagine how others afford to either."

"Maybe they don't," I said thoughtfully. "Maybe that's just how it goes in the game of snooker—a fact of life. I never practised either… not really. I just got what little practice I could from playing. Until I came here, that is."

Then I smiled. “Actually, because of how successful this practice has been, I’ve updated the old saying. It’s no longer ‘Practice makes perfect.’ I now say, *‘Perfect practising makes perfection.’*”

Frank chuckled softly, but then shifted the conversation.

“John, to change the subject… You never did tell me how you managed to come on a two-year holiday from prison. Good for you, though.”

“Not that it helps you any, Frank,” I said, “but honestly, I don’t know why they didn’t send me back to that hell of a place. I asked the Governor the same thing. He said he didn’t know either.”

“Would it have anything to do with that *other* thing you haven’t told me?”

“What other thing?”

“The reason for your accident. Why weren’t you paying attention when driving such a massive lorry?”

I paused. “No… I haven’t told anyone about that. It’s… it’s a very embarrassing matter.”

Frank gave me a small nod, not pushing further. “Well, whatever it is… Let’s go. Susan’s waiting for you.”

β

As Frank drove me to Susan’s house, I sat in silence, feeling sick with myself. That morning, I’d treated my brother the way I had been treated in *real* prison—overpowering him, belittling him, even if it was only through snooker.

I knew it at the time. I should have stopped. But I didn't. I let the thrill of showing off take over.

Worse still, I'd lied to him. I *had* told Brian the real reason I wanted to understand how the brain works during snooker.

Turning to Frank, I finally said, "Let's not play snooker next Saturday. Instead… let me show you what I've learned. I want to help you improve—properly—the way Brian helped me."

Chapter 11

Using My Sight and Touch Together

The next day—Sunday—I spent the entire day trying to progress from just potting a ball to practising how to build a break. I used only the cue ball, a red, and the black. My goal was simple: pot the red ball, then apply just the right weight of touch on the cue ball so it would roll forward and stop close enough to the black for a follow-up shot.

I wanted to see whether I could consistently use my sense of *touch*, in addition to *sight*, to control the outcome—the only two senses my brain allowed in that task: SIGHT and TOUCH!

After enough time at the table, I glanced over at the dartboard that had been staring me in the face for weeks. I'd never taken much interest in darts before, but a question struck me: could *Persistent Eye Fixation* apply there too?

What senses would I need to use to perform well in darts? Sight and touch—the same as snooker! And the task? Think of the screams in professional matches when all three darts land in treble twenty. "One hundred and eighty!" they shout. To land all three darts in that tiny segment must take *hours and hours* of practice—and surely, it must involve persistent eye fixation, helping the brain store the memory of that perfect throw.

Wow. The more I thought about it, the more I realised just how powerful this concept was—across all sports requiring precision.

ß

The next day—Monday—I popped into Brian's office, eager to tell him how well I'd been doing since last Wednesday.

I told him I'd spent all of Thursday and Friday practising persistent eye fixation—locking onto the target spot on the object ball. I felt like my brain was *helping* me. As if it was downloading the memory of the previous shot within just a few seconds. It was magical.

But then I sighed. "Oh Brian, Saturday morning was pathetic. I completely showed off to Frank… and I hurt him, badly. He's agreed to come again next Saturday, to let me teach him—but I honestly don't know how we'll fill three hours doing that. I worry he won't want to come back after that."

Brian gave me a look of encouragement. "And what about Sunday's long practice? What did you work on then?"

"I moved on to practising making breaks," I said. I told him everything I'd done with the red and black.

He nodded and said, "Here's an idea. Break up your session with Frank by alternating between short lessons and quick games. Use just three red balls instead of fifteen—that way, the games won't take too long. Even if he loses easily, explain to him beforehand how you're approaching each shot. Tell him how you fixate your eyes and what your plan is for the break."

He smiled. "That way, Frank can learn to copy your successes—especially when it comes to controlling the *weight* of the shot. Remember, you once told me that both of you used to hit the cue ball so hard it would zip around the table twice and land itself in a pocket!"

I laughed. "Yeah, we've come a long way since then."

Chapter 12

Susan's Sunday Surprise

The following Saturday was simply amazing. I had been worried about what Frank and I would do to fill the time after our snooker session—but I needn't have. We couldn't stop playing! We used just three reds instead of the usual fifteen, as Brian had suggested. It worked beautifully. So well, in fact, that we ended up playing all day. But… a big, big *BUT*… I couldn't go to Susan's that evening!

Over supper, the Governor said I could use his phone to call her—though he made it clear not to make a habit of it.

When I got through, her voice cut in sharply: "Stuff your practising. I need you tomorrow. I'll pick you up after breakfast at nine."

Interesting.

I tried talking to her during the drive, but she didn't say a word. Still, she had a huge grin on her face, so I didn't mind the quiet ride.

Once we arrived at her house, I noticed a man's suit laid out on her bed.

"Hmm…"

"Frank lent you that," she said casually. "Did you know you're the same height and weight as your brother?"

"Yes," I said, "but why would he want me to wear his suit? I've never worn one in my life—I'm a lorry driver!"

Then I joked, "You're not taking me to church, are you?"

She smiled. "Very sharp. That's exactly where we're going. I want to know what it feels like to be in a church… *before* you marry me."

β

For the next month or so, I was happier than I had ever been.

Frank and I played snooker all day on Saturdays—still using our new three-red system—and I spent Sundays with Susan. Not in church after that first visit, but with her family: joining them for Sunday roasts at the local pub, walking in the countryside, playing card games, and occasionally (though not my favourite), Monopoly.

Life was finally beginning to feel… whole.

Then everything changed again.

"Smith," the Governor called. "We have a visitor for you. Please come with me to the office."

Who could that be?

β

As I entered the Governor's office,a middle-aged woman stood up and approached me with a warm smile, holding out her hand.

The Governor introduced me. "This is John Smith."

She nodded. "Janet Jones. Please, call me Janet."

We shook hands. Then she and I sat facing each other while the Governor took his seat behind his desk.

She seems like someone of class, I thought. *Is 'Janet Jones' a pseudonym?*

She spoke gently. "You're probably wondering who I am."

"I am," I admitted.

"It was my husband who died in the accident."

In an instant, **his tortured eyes flashed before me—staring up through his windscreen, moments before impact.**

I couldn't hold it together. I ran from the room, tears splashing to the floor.

β

When I returned, the Governor and Ms. Jones sat waiting, both still smiling softly.

I took a deep breath and said, "Please listen to me, Mrs. Jones. I wanted to say—to you and your family—that I was so, so sorry for my criminal act. But I was too much of a coward to say it at the time. I never sought forgiveness because I didn't deserve it. Even now, I feel like saying 'sorry' is completely inadequate. I don't know what else to say… but I am still very, very sorry."

To my surprise, Janet was still smiling—and so was the Governor.

"John," she said gently, "I've come to bring you *good news*. That's why we're smiling. But first, I'd like to know just one thing—before I tell you my story.

What was it you were thinking about that caused your inattentiveness while driving? You'd driven perfectly for ten years. Why that one moment?"

I paused. Then she added, "How could a world champion snooker player miss a sitter?"

I sighed. "I've been trying to figure that out ever since—but with no success."

She leaned forward slightly. "Let me tell you *my* story then."

CHAPTER 13
The Enlightenment

"First of all," she began gently, "my name isn't actually Janet Jones. That's just for security reasons. But please trust what I'm about to tell you—everything is the truth.

"My husband worked in the securities industry and travelled all over the country on business. When the accident happened, the police investigated thoroughly. They concluded that because it was rush hour and he was driving in the outside lane, he couldn't avoid going under the lorry. He had been driving for many years without ever causing an accident. Naturally, we—the family—were devastated. And at the time, I don't think any of us would have welcomed you with the smile I offer today.

"My husband was always very mindful of the dangers of driving. In fact, he had a habit—whenever someone new got into his car, he would say, *'If I don't answer a question you ask me, it's because I'm paying attention to the traffic.'*

"But I've thought about the accident over and over again. What he may not have considered was the possibility that the brake lights coming on in the inside lanes had anything to do with him. After all, there was a clear road ahead—nothing visible to warn him. He might have assumed, wrongly, that any issue in the inner lanes wouldn't affect him in the outside lane. If that's what happened… well, it *could* be classed as inattentiveness on his part too, don't you think?"

She paused, then continued: "I put these thoughts to the authorities. But they said that all the legal evidence was against *you* and that nothing could be done about changing the sentence.

"Then I spoke to your employer. He mentioned your obsession with snooker—how you were desperate to watch the World Snooker Championship. He said he'd heard of a player missing a sitter, which you would find it hard to understand why. That's when I guessed what must have distracted you that day… and I was right.

"The authorities must have also thought about it—and likely worried about your mental state. Perhaps they feared what might happen to you in prison. Things like rape… suicide. Not something they wanted on their hands. So, they agreed to send you here."

β

"Do you have any questions?" she asked.

I swallowed, still overwhelmed. "Yes. I'm wondering why you've come to tell me all this. But thank you… already, thank you for what you've done for me!"

"We're getting to that," she smiled. "I came here because I've heard about your progress—your success with snooker. And I wondered… have you thought about turning professional?"

I blinked. "No… I haven't. Right now, I'm just half-decent as an amateur. Going pro takes years of training, real coaching, and you have to be *very* good."

"But does the idea appeal to you?"

"Oh yes," I breathed. "Wow. That would be… incredible. Why do you ask?"

"Because," she said, her voice calm but full of conviction, "if you're truly interested, then I want to sponsor you. Some of my husband's wealth—now passed down to me—will be used to fund your training and development. I will be your sponsor… and your friend. Or, more accurately, *my husband's money* will make it possible. And I believe—in my heart—that he would have wanted this.

"I've already agreed with the authorities to take responsibility for the rest of your service time. I'll arrange accommodation and finance as many training sessions and tournaments as you wish to attend—anywhere in the UK. And I'll sponsor you for at least five years beyond your release."

The Governor, grinning from ear to ear, added, "Just don't forget to be back by ten!"

I couldn't hold it in any longer. Tears of joy streamed down my face.

Sequel

Susan and I were married in a quiet, beautiful ceremony. She continued living with her family for the time being, while I remained at the Open Prison—travelling frequently for competitions and training courses. When I was back, I made good use of the snooker facilities there, which now felt more like a second home than a place of confinement.

Over time, my game improved beyond anything I'd imagined. I turned out to be a genuinely strong snooker player—and next year, I'll be competing in the *World Championships* in the North of England.

Wish me luck.

APPENDIX 1

Definitions With Author's Note

- **Eye Fixations** in sports are essential for achieving peak performance. Your brain only accepts sensory input relevant to the task—everything else is "noise" and can degrade your performance. In snooker, darts, football, and golf, only *sight* and *touch* are essential. Smell, taste, and hearing? Just noise.
- **Persistent Eye Fixation** refers to holding your gaze, steadily and intentionally, on a precise point—often for seconds or split seconds or even longer, 'IF PRACTISING'.
- **"On that shot"** refers to the moment the cue strikes the cue ball.
- **"The sitter"** means an easy shot—one you'd expect to pot.
- **"Potted"** is when a shot is successfully made—the object ball is sunk into a pocket.
- **Insomnia** is a sleep disorder involving difficulty falling asleep, staying asleep, or waking up too early (referenced in Appendix 4).

Appendix 2

Links To Darts, Football and Golf

1. Darts

In darts, *Eye Fixation* is the final concentrated gaze on a target—bullseye, treble twenty, etc.—just before the throwing action begins. This skill directly correlates with accuracy and is discussed further in Chapter 11.

2. Football

In football, *Eye Fixation* is used to focus attention and extract visual information for decision-making.

Example: Taking a penalty.

Persistent Eye Fixation is key. You lock your focus on a point—like the foot of a goalpost or the top corner—and block out everything else, including the goalkeeper. The beauty lies in your ability to adapt even in the final second, thanks to well-practised fixation.

Other uses:

- When shooting from distance, fixate on the inside of the post.
- When shooting in motion, use repetition and practice to instinctively apply fixation along specific lines and angles.

And yes, I've groaned along with the crowd when players miss 'sitters'—goals that looked easier to score than miss!

3. Golf

In golf, Eye Fixation is typically on the back of the ball during a putt. The golfer fixates with their dominant eye, letting peripheral vision manage the rest—distance, line, terrain.

This fixation helps:

- Control the club through impact
- Maintain hand-eye coordination
- Execute calm, precise movement under pressure

4. Snooker

Snooker is as much a psychological game as a physical one. It demands strategy, composure, and relentless focus.

Watching professionals on TV offers great insight. Observe the entire process—from when they begin fixating on the shot, to the final pot. Watch how they transition between shots, especially during break-building. Practice alone to internalize these techniques.

A practical tip: If, like me, you wear glasses, the top rim may interfere with your line of sight. Try *snooker glasses*, designed with this issue in mind. Search online—or email me for a personal recommendation.

Appendix 3

The Author's Personal Link To The Story

1. The Awful Accident

The dramatic accident described in the story—mirrors a real one I experienced on the M1 while returning from a meeting in Wolverhampton.

2. My Real-Life Crash

It was a February evening, snow falling but not settling—just being crushed into cold slush by traffic. I was in the outside lane at about 60mph. No cars ahead, clear road. Then, brake lights lit up in the inner lanes. I assumed it wasn't my concern. I was wrong.

Suddenly, I was heading straight toward a lorry's front. No time to swerve. I braked hard, knowing I was going under. For three or four seconds, I thought I was about to die.

Then… blackout.

I awoke in an ambulance on the hard shoulder. Bandaged, but no real pain. I refused hospital and got dropped at Birmingham New Street, then took a train back to London.

Later, I received a notice that the lorry driver was fined £100 for dangerous driving. No cheque came with it—not that it mattered.

My car's design saved me: in a head-on crash, the bonnet lifted over the windscreen, and the engine dropped to the ground instead of ramming back into the cabin.

For months, I had nightmares. But strangely, since then, I've never truly felt stress. Whenever pressure looms, I think: *"I shouldn't even be here. So how important is this, really?"*

APPENDIX 4

Author's Extras — Sleep & Fixation

Can Persistent Fixation help with sleep?

Absolutely. While writing this story, I often went to bed late—tired but unable to sleep. My mind was buzzing with plot points and tomorrow's to-do list.

That mental chatter? That's **noise**. And fixation can help shut it down.

Here's how I do it:

- Close your eyes.
- Fixate your mind on one thing: the task of going to sleep.
- Eliminate the "noise."

Focus solely on the sound of your breathing—slow, steady, natural. Persist.

Eventually, you'll drift off—though you won't know exactly when. But who cares? You'll wake up feeling rested.

Sometimes it fails. If it does, repeat. Kick out the noise. Stay with your breath. And… *zzzzzzzz.*

P.S. It works during the day too—I take afternoon naps regularly (okay, most days!).

ANOTHER AUTHOR'S BOOK

In This 'Self Help Series':

Title: *Why Do You Drink So Much?*

Subtitle: *Avoiding Alcoholism Wins!*

Why Do You Drink So Much? is a fictional story centred around the theme of avoiding the slippery slope into alcoholism.

Pam and Steven are a happily married couple—until Steven's drinking starts to take a toll on their lives. Told from Pam's perspective, the story draws you into her emotional world: the love, the frustration, the fear, and the heartbreak of watching someone you care deeply about lose control.

You'll feel the weight of her words when she finally says: **"I love you so much, Steven, but I have nothing left to do but abandon you. What are you going to do, my love, my darling?"**

But no, no, no… that's **not** the end.

This story is deeply personal. It's inspired by my own experience of quitting alcohol overnight—twenty years ago—after finding a simple message from my wife left on the breakfast table: **"Why do you drink so much?"**

That question changed everything. Had I ignored it, I might have lasted five more years as an alcoholic. I might also have lost my family, my dignity, and my health. Instead, I made a different choice. And this story explores how that turning point can happen—before it's too late.

Appendices:

- My personal connection to the story as the author
- Exploring links between major addictions
- How to contact the author

READERS' COMMENT

"Your theory and explanation on the subject you aimed at—Eye Fixation—is brilliant."

"This is an enjoyable mystery story built around the theme of Eye Fixation in sport. It reminded me of my own golf-playing days—sadly behind me now. It was difficult to put the story down. I read it three times."

"A very enjoyable read, with a mystery storyline woven into practical advice for sportsmen."

"Eye Fixation for sports performance, enveloped in a great 'Howdunnit' mystery—what a combination!"

"It's been a long time since I played snooker, though I enjoy watching it on TV. I wish I'd had this valuable information about Eye Fixation back then. I remember so clearly saying, *'What if I miss?'***—and choosing a safety shot instead. And yes, it was a seemingly easy shot... but I didn't want to leave it open for my opponent."**

Printed in Dunstable, United Kingdom

64844293R00029